EVERYDAY

Blessings

Spiritual Refreshment for Women

REBECCA CURRINGTON

BARBOUR
PUBLISHING

ISBN 978-1-59789-660-3

Cover design © Kirk DouPonce, www.DogEaredDesign.com

Writing and compilation: Rebecca Currington, Debbie Kubik Evert, Shanna Gregor, and Carol Smith in association with Snapdragon Group℠ Editorial Services.

Published by Barbour Publishing, Inc., P.O. Box 719, Uhrichsville, Ohio 44683.

Our mission is to publish and distribute inspirational products offering exceptional value and biblical encouragement to the masses.

Printed in India.

Contents

Every good and perfect gift
is from above, coming
down from the Father
of the heavenly lights,
who does not change
like shifting shadows.

JAMES 1:17

Introduction

Blessings are God's gifts to us—simple
or great, they are produced by the overflow of His great love. We recognize these
most often when they include a reprieve
from sickness or a financial provision for
a critical need. But we are prone to take for
granted the sunshine that lights our days
and lifts our spirits, the affection of friends
and family, the kindness of strangers.

Everyday Blessings was created to open
your eyes to the blessings all around
you, to encourage you to bask
in the lovingkindness of our
awesome God. It is our prayer
that as you move through

these pages, you will see God's hand in every
aspect of your life, filling it with goodness,
hope, joy, and peace.

Abilities

We have different gifts,
according to the grace given us.

ROMANS 12:6

God has blessed every person—every single one—with some gift or ability with which to serve others and bring glory to His name. Some abilities are obvious—they shine brightly in front of everyone—but others move below the radar. They include things like the ability to pray effectively, love the unlovely, listen attentively. Ask God to open your eyes to your special abilities. They are God's blessings to you.

Do not neglect your gift. . . .
Be diligent in these matters;
give yourself wholly to them, so that
everyone may see your progress.

I TIMOTHY 4:14–15

The Bible most often refers to human abilities as gifts because they are given in order to be given again. If you have the gift of song, God expects you to strengthen and polish that gift and use it to enrich the lives of others. If you have been given a way with children, extend that gift to every child you meet. As you use your gifts to bless others, you will be blessed most of all.

Abundance

Rejoice in the LORD your God, for he has given you the autumn rains in righteousness. He sends you abundant showers, both autumn and spring rains.

JOEL 2:23

As human beings, we are limited in what we can provide for those we love—our resources, both material and emotional, are finite. But God has no limits. He blesses His children far beyond our comprehension. He does more than just rain down His blessings on us; He sends abundant showers of blessing in every season of our lives. You are a rich woman. Once you see all God has provided for you, you won't ever want to come in out of the rain.

Grace and peace be yours
in abundance.

1 PETER 1:2

As you look around at God's blessings in your life, close your eyes and look inward, as well. God has also provided you with an abundance of grace and peace. Grace that allows you to be who you genuinely are and the peace of knowing that who you are is just fine with Him. Women are wonderfully emotional people, the keepers of the inner life. If your inner places are dark and empty, invite God to fill them to overflowing with His goodness.

Acceptance

[God] chose us in Him before the
foundation of the world. . .according
to the good pleasure of His will,
to the praise of the glory of His grace,
by which He made us accepted
in the Beloved.

EPHESIANS 1:4–6 NKJV

You may never receive the full acceptance
and approval of the people in your life. But
God has already given you His approval, His
acceptance. He chose you. Think about that.
Almighty God chose you! No one compelled
Him to. His motive wasn't pity. The Bible
says He created you and pronounced His
work "good." He's proud of the "you" He's
made, and He is moved with love for you—
just as you are.

> Honor God by accepting each other,
> as Christ has accepted you.
>
> ROMANS 15:7 CEV

Just as God has accepted you, He asks that you accept others. That doesn't mean you must accept their aberrant behaviors or keep your mouth shut when you see people doing things they shouldn't. Accepting others means appreciating that each person was created by and is loved by God. They have value for that reason. In loving Him, you must love whom He loves and accept whom He accepts. That's the only proper response to so great a Creator.

Accomplishment

A longing fulfilled is a tree of life.
PROVERBS 13:12

You are a fortunate woman! You live in a
time when women can accomplish anything
they set their minds to do. Are there still
obstacles? Of course, but nothing you can't
deal with. God has given you something
special to do in this world. You'll know it by
the longing you feel deep inside. Ask God to
guide you, lending you His wisdom, grace,
and strength. Then go for it. Nothing can
compare with the joy of accomplishing God's will for your life.

> Commit your work to the Lord, and
> your plans will be established.
>
> PROVERBS 16:3 NRSV

Whatever God has called you to accomplish in your life, He has not called you to accomplish alone. He is always there, providing you with the resources you need to get the job done. That doesn't mean you won't stumble along the way or encounter difficulties. But it does mean that you can call upon the counsel and resources of almighty God to help you. Whether you need wisdom, inspiration, confidence, strength, or just plain tenacity, you will find your answer in Him.

Ambition

Stand firm. Let nothing move you.
Always give yourselves fully
to the work of the Lord,
because you know that your labor
in the Lord is not in vain.

1 CORINTHIANS 15:58

Simply defined, ambition means determination to succeed. That's a positive thing—essential, in fact, to accomplishing God's will and purpose for your life. It helps you look past the obstacles in your path—age, health, education, lack of finances, etc.—to the prize waiting on the other side. God wants you to be determined, even ambitious. He's given you that inner motivation to help you complete the task He's assigned to you. Thank Him for it!

16

> Do nothing out of selfish ambition
> or vain conceit, but in humility
> consider others better than yourself.
>
> PHILIPPIANS 2:3

Ambition is a positive characteristic—
unless it begins to take over your life. Are
you pursuing your goals—even God-given
goals—at the expense of others? Out of
control, ambition can cause you to do things
you would never do otherwise. God expects
you to couple your ambition with godliness.
Only then will you truly be accomplishing
His will for you. Only then will you truly
fulfill the desires He has placed in your
heart.

Appearance

What matters is not your outer appearance—the styling of your hair, the jewelry you wear, the cut of your clothes—but your inner disposition. Cultivate inner beauty, the gentle, gracious kind that God delights in.

1 PETER 3:3-4 MSG

Most women care how they look. That's why they carry mirrors in their purses and purchase billions of dollars of makeup each year. There's nothing wrong with looking good on the outside as long as you remember to primp and preen your inner self, as well. God wants your beauty to be more than skin deep. He wants it to be heart deep. Work to be as fully beautiful as you were created to be.

The LORD does not look
at the things man looks at.
Man looks at the outward appearance,
but the LORD looks at the heart.

1 SAMUEL 16:7

When God looks at you, He sees a
beautiful woman, a temple worthy of His
Spirit. He sees your virtuous life and
your godly attitudes. He sees a person
whose heart has been washed clean and
fully submitted to His will and purpose.
He sees a beauty that is often missed by
others. He sees an inner beauty that
transcends any physical characteristics—
good or bad. God sees you as you really are.

Armor of God

Put on the full armor of God
so that you can take your stand
against the devil's schemes.

EPHESIANS 6:11

It's a good idea for every woman to take a
basic class in self-defense in order to protect herself in this predator-filled world. A
wise woman will learn how to defend herself
spiritually, as well. God has provided you
with a full suit of armor for that purpose—
truth, righteousness, peace, faith, and salvation. Wear them everywhere you go. You do
have an enemy, and he wants to take all you
have. Be prepared to resist and defeat him.

Our struggle is not against flesh
and blood, but against the rulers,
against the authorities,
against the powers of this dark world
and against the spiritual forces
of evil in the heavenly realms.

EPHESIANS 6:12

In God's kingdom, women are called to
be warriors. Alongside their Christian
brothers, they are asked to battle with the
forces of evil that plot to destroy human
lives and keep them from knowing their
Creator. This is a warfare fought in spiritual
realms with an enemy we know is there but
cannot see. Put on your spiritual armor and
ask God to point out your battle station.
And then—on to victory!

Assurance

When my skin sags
and my bones get brittle,
God is rock-firm and faithful.

PSALM 73:26 MSG

It's the nature of a woman to need
assurance—confirmation that she is pretty
enough, smart enough, pleasing enough.
God wants you to know that "you are more
than enough!" He is pleased with you. He
wants you to be assured that He will always
be there for you. You need not fear that He
will grow tired of you, lose interest, and
abandon you. You are precious to
Him, no matter your age, your
condition, your circumstances.
You matter to Him.

God affirms us, making us a sure thing
in Christ, putting his Yes within us.
By his Spirit he has stamped us with his
eternal pledge—a sure beginning
of what he is destined to complete.

2 CORINTHIANS 1:21–22 MSG

The last time you bought a house or a car or
applied for a loan, were you preapproved?
Good feeling, isn't it? In a real sense,
you have been preapproved for God's
kingdom. He's given you His Word and
stamped you with His eternal pledge. You
belong to Him. He is fully committed to
helping you become all you were created
to be. You can turn your back on Him—it's
true. But He will never turn His back on you.

Attitude

Be constantly renewed in the spirit
of your mind [having a fresh mental
and spiritual attitude].

EPHESIANS 4:23 AMP

Your attitude can substantially affect your
happiness level. It's true. When your mind is
assaulted every day by "stinkin' thinkin'"—
things like, "I'm not good enough," "I'm not
loved," "I'll never reach my dreams"—it's
pretty tough to be happy. On the other hand,
when you think about good things—God
things—your happiness level will soar. Try it!
"God loves me," "God is always by my side,
watching out for me," "God has made me a
winner." What a difference it will make.

Put off your old self, which is being
corrupted by its deceitful desires;
to be made new in the attitude of
your minds; and to put on the new self,
created to be like God in true
righteousness and holiness.

EPHESIANS 4:22–24

The key to a great attitude is to rise above
your old ways of thinking and start thinking
like God thinks. The Bible says we aren't
capable of thinking God's actual thoughts.
They are too high and holy. But you can
think like God—raising your mind-sight to
focus on the good, the right, the holy, helping and encouraging others, ways to express
your thankfulness. An attitude is simply a
response to what you see—keep your mind
tuned in to the good.

Belief

He that cometh to God must believe
that he is, and that he is a rewarder
of them that diligently seek him.

HEBREWS 11:6 KJV

Belief is one of those things you can't see
physically, but you still have it. For example,
you believe a chair will hold you when you
sit in it. You can't explain the physics of it,
but you sit in it believing it will do what it's
supposed to do. Belief in God is like that. You
put your trust in Him that He will do what He
said He would do. The Bible, His written
word, is filled with those promises.

On the last and greatest day of the Feast,
Jesus stood and said in a loud voice,
"If anyone is thirsty, let him come to me
and drink. Whoever believes in me, as
the Scripture has said, streams of living
water will flow from within him."

JOHN 7:37–38

Ever been so thirsty nothing can quench
your thirst? You're desperate to find res-
olution. You try everything within reach.
You even try substitutes, but they're just that:
a substitution for the real thing. Sometimes we aren't just physically thirsty, but
we have that deep-down soul-type thirst.
You're seeking something in your life that
will completely quench your parched soul.
Jesus said that only He can satisfy that kind of
thirst. He's there, no waiting. He can fill your
life to overflowing.

Bible

Your word is a lamp to my feet
and a light for my path.

PSALM 119:105

If only life came with an instruction
manual, you've said to yourself. Help for
when you don't know what to do. The Bible
is filled with stories of ordinary people
who lived through struggles and triumphs,
heartache and joy. Unlike the stories we see
today on television, not every story has a
happy ending. People saw consequences of
their erroneous actions. Through it all, God
shines a light for our paths today.

The word of God is living and active.
Sharper than any double-edged sword,
it penetrates even to dividing soul and
spirit, joints and marrow; it judges the
thoughts and attitudes of the heart.

HEBREWS 4:12

The Bible is God's love letter to you. It isn't
the sappy romance novel found in drug-
stores. The characters in those stories give
only conditional love to each other. God's
love is unconditional. From the first words
in the book of Genesis, where God created
the heavens and the earth, He is commu-
nicating His love to you. It's the love letter
you've longed to read. Open it up and see
for yourself.

Burdens

Jesus said, "Come to me all you
who are weary and burdened,
and I will give you rest."

MATTHEW 11:28

Weary. Burdened. Need rest. Those words
read like a repeating entry in a woman's daily
journal. Most women feel they've earned the
right to be burdened. What else but weary
could they be with all they have to do? Jesus
said that He would give rest to those who are
weary. He would lighten our loads. Take one
burden at a time and hand it over to
Him. And then rest in the peace that
Jesus has our lives in the palm of
His hands.

Carry each other's burdens,
and in this way you will
fulfill the law of Christ.

GALATIANS 6:2

Have you seen the size of kids' backpacks
lately? Their backs sway with the weight of
books, papers, and "stuff." Kids carry these
packs all day on their tired shoulders.
Relief comes when they drop the
weighty bags at home. The burdens
you carry around each day may be caus-
ing your shoulders to droop, as well. Take
those worries and burdens to God. He
has promised to lighten your load by
adding His shoulder to yours.

Challenge

Because the Sovereign LORD helps me,
I will not be disgraced. Therefore
have I set my face like flint, and
I know I will not be put to shame.

ISAIAH 50:7

Life is full of challenges. While some are
short-term, others last a lifetime. What
keeps you determined and motivated? Do
you seek the help of others or prefer to go
it alone? Take a toddler's approach to these
challenges. As she ventures into walking,
she takes one step at a time, with help from a
steady adult or an available piece of furni-
ture. Eventually, she walks on her own. With
God's help, take life's challenges one step at
a time.

> Let us run with endurance
> the race that is set before us,
> looking unto Jesus, the author
> and finisher of our faith.
>
> HEBREWS 12:1–2 NKJV

Do you ever get tired of life's challenges? Do you wish you could live a carefree, predictable life? While that isn't possible, you can have a different perspective on the challenges that come your way. The Bible says we will encounter trials in this life. After all, this world is not our home; it's just a temporary residence. While we are here, though, God promised His presence, love, and comfort. He will walk beside you and give you strength to overcome whatever is in your path.

Change

Jesus Christ is the same yesterday
and today and forever.

HEBREWS 13:8 NASB

Your schedule fluctuates from day to day,
and you have the calendar to prove it.
Decades ago, life was pretty much the same
every day, especially for women. Most of
what we did was for others: church and
big family dinners on Sundays, wash on
Mondays, ironing on Tuesdays, etc. Aren't
you glad you live in a time when you can
experience new things every day? As
you long for consistency, look to
Jesus. His loving character never
changes. He was, is, and will be.

If anyone is in Christ,
he is a new creation;
the old has gone, the new has come!

2 CORINTHIANS 5:17

The monarch butterfly begins life as a lowly worm. Through the course of time, it makes itself a cocoon and eventually turns into a beautiful butterfly. Similarly, we come to Christ with the potential to be a beautiful butterfly. Through challenges and normal life events, we go through a spiritual metamorphosis and become new creatures. We are free to fly and be what God intended us to be. His intention for you is beauty and grace. Trust Him to see you through the transformation.

Character

[The Lord] guides the humble in what
is right and teaches them his way.

PSALM 25:9

The phrase "We're known by the com-
pany we keep" is true regardless of whom
you hang around with. It's also true when
it's God you're spending time with. As you
rest in His presence, read His words in the
Bible, and talk to Him about all the issues of
your life, you cannot help but take on some
of His characteristics. He is peace, and you
become more peaceful. He is good, and you
take on His goodness. It's all about the com-
pany you keep.

We show we are servants of God
by our pure lives.

2 CORINTHIANS 6:6 NCV

Character has been defined as what one is. It's the very essence of a person. The Bible says a lot about God's character and uses phrases such as "God is love"; "God is compassionate"; "God is merciful." His actions show His character. When we belong to God, we reflect His character: We are kind, loving, caring, compassionate. Our actions and behaviors reflect that character: We love, we care, we serve.

Charity

Happy are those who are
kind to the poor.

PROVERBS 14:21 NRSV

You see people in need almost every day.
Whether they are hungry or hurting, the
Bible says to give out of the overflow of love
you have received from God. He will work
through you as you serve food to those who
are hungry, give clothing to those who need
covering, offer hope to those who feel hope-
less. You can serve them with gentle words
and kind deeds. Serving the powerless
is a blessing in itself, but it carries a
bonus—God's eternal reward.

Jesus said, "I tell you the truth, whatever you did for one of the least of these brothers of mine, you did for me."

MATTHEW 25:40

What would you do if Jesus came to your house for dinner? Although you might be nervous, He would want you to be yourself, to serve Him as you would any other guest. You would give Him the best you have, out of the abundance He has provided for you. It would not matter what was served, but He would delight in your efforts on His behalf. Jesus is pleased when you serve others as you would serve Him.

Children

If any of you lacks wisdom,
he should ask God, who gives
generously to all without finding fault,
and it will be given to him.

JAMES 1:5

You can read books and ask others for advice as you raise your children, but how can you be assured what you're doing is the best for them? Just as your children come to you with questions, take your questions to God, your heavenly Father. No question is too small or too big. You can't stump Him, because He knows you and your children intimately. After all, He has created you all. God is the best resource you can find.

Children are a gift from God;
they are his reward.

PSALM 127:3 TLB

If you're a mother, you know how precious
your children are to you. They are bone of
your bone, flesh of your flesh. You would
not hesitate to protect them with your life.
And well you should, for that's your job.
Take a moment to remember that you are
God's child, created in His own image.
He gave His very life to save you, and even
now He hovers over you protectively. Your
children are God's gift to you. You are God's
gift to Himself.

Choices

Choose life and not death!
2 KINGS 18:32

No matter how good—or bad—your choices have been in your life, there is really just one choice that matters. That is the choice of where you will spend eternity. God has given you a free will, and He expects you to use it. You must choose Him—consciously, intentionally choose Him—or you will be making a choice by default, a choice against Him. The Bible says it's a life and death matter. Your free will is His gift to you—use it!

Choose this day whom you will serve. . .
but as for me and my household,
we will serve the Lord.

JOSHUA 24:15 NRSV

From the mundane to the life-altering, we make choices every day. Do you wish you could see into the future and know which direction your life will take if you make this or that choice? Perhaps it's for the best that we don't have that option. But you can put your trust in the One who does. Listen to the Lord; choose Him. When you do, it will be much easier to make the right choices for your life.

Comfort

The Lord will hear your crying,
and he will comfort you.
When he hears you, he will help you.

ISAIAH 30:19 NCV

The Christian life is difficult—and emotional. It was for Jesus' disciples also. Jesus knew His death would be the most emotional moment of their lives. So just before Jesus gave His life on the cross, He sat down with them, explained that He would be leaving, and promised that He would send another "Comforter," the Holy Spirit. He has placed His Comforter inside of you. He hears every cry.

> Whatsoever things were written aforetime were written for our learning, that we through patience and comfort of the scriptures might have hope.
>
> ROMANS 15:4 KJV

God has given you another gift filled with His love and comfort—the holy scriptures. As you read about Noah, Abraham, Jacob, Joseph, Moses, Esther, Ruth, Job, David, Elijah, Mary, and Paul, you will see how God comforted them in their darkest hours. He will certainly do the same for you. Be encouraged as you read, and place your hope in His goodness. He will comfort you, and you can be sure of that.

Commitment

"Your hearts must be fully
committed to the LORD our God,
to live by his decrees and obey
his commands, as at this time."

I KINGS 8:61

Many women have issues with commitment. Their fear of failure causes them to
drift in and out of relationships, jobs, and
obligations without ever really settling anywhere. Committing your life first to God will
help you commit later to others. Give Him
your love, your life, your heart, and ask Him
to help you walk out your commitment one day at a time. Everything
else will follow.

Commit everything you do to the Lord.
PSALM 37:5 TLB

Some women can't commit, while others overcommit. Even when your intentions are good, you can bring down your whole house of cards by trying to juggle too many things—family, social events, work, spiritual time. Soon you find yourself with no per-sonal time, becoming more stressed by the moment. Ask God to help you bal-ance your commitments in a way that is healthy for you. Then you will be free to meet your commitments head-on and accomplish them with excellence.

Compassion

You, O Lord, are a compassionate
and gracious God, slow to anger,
abounding in love and faithfulness.

God never asks you to do anything for
someone else that He has not already done
for you. You are able to show compassion
for others because He has shown compassion for you. When you were lost and lonely,
He found you. When you were sick with
sin, He forgave you. When your life was in
shambles, He held you close and comforted
you. When you longed for a fresh start, He
opened the way before you. You give from
what you have already received.

Never walk away from someone
who deserves help;
your hand is God's hand
for that person.

PROVERBS 3:28 MSG

The Bible reminds us that we are God's
hands and feet. We carry His compassion
to the world around us. What a wonderful
privilege and responsibility. Ask God to
open your eyes to the people around you
who need His merciful touch, His gentle
encouragement, His tender intervention.
You won't be able to meet all the needs you
see, but if you're asking, He will show you
where you can make a difference. And when
you raise another's head, you raise your
own, as well.

Confidence

In quietness and in confidence
shall be your strength.

ISAIAH 30:15 KJV

Confidence is really just the quiet assurance
that you are enough—enough of an employee
to get the job done, enough of a wife and
mother to take care of your family, enough
of a woman of God to accomplish what
He's called you to do. For some women, that
comes easily, for others, not so much. If your
confidence is lagging, reach out to God for
help. He will help you unveil the real
you—the confident and assured you.

Such confidence as this is ours
through Christ before God.
Not that we are competent in
ourselves to claim anything
for ourselves, but our
competence comes from God.

2 CORINTHIANS 3:4–5

As a child of God, you should be confident about who you are—not pushy or
overbearing—a woman who knows
she is the daughter of a great and
mighty king. Draw your confidence from
your relationship with your heavenly
Father; then take life one challenge at
a time. It isn't about being perfect. It's
about being sure of whom you believe in
and who you are in Him.

Contentment

I say it is better to be content with
what little you have. Otherwise,
you will always be struggling for more,
and that is like chasing the wind.

ECCLESIASTES 4:6 NCV

When it comes to evaluating your life,
God's scales weigh differently than yours.
Seeing through His eyes, the smallest
things can bring you the deepest joy. When
you embrace your life just as it is, you can
lay down the struggle for what might be or
might have been. You can feel the blessing of
contentment that, for this moment, your life
is the perfect starting place for the next step
in the journey.

I have learned to be content
with whatever I have.

PHILIPPIANS 4:11 NRSV

Having what you want, or wanting what
you have. It's amazing what a difference
the order of those simple words can make.
What a gift it is to feel that sense of enough,
to not always be thinking more, to believe
that God has given what you truly need. As
you focus today on the pockets of your life
that you "wouldn't have any other way,"
whisper a prayer of thanks. Take a breath
and let this moment be full, just on its own.

Courage

Lord, you are my shield, my wonderful
God who gives me courage.

PSALM 3:3 NCV

You never know where courage will pop up
in your life, because you never know what
you'll face that will require it. You can be
sure, though, that God will give you courage
when you need it. God is both your protec-
tor and your strength. So be confident that
whatever you face, you do not face it alone.
You face today with resources both from
your own soul and the Spirit that
dwells within you.

Jesus said, "In the world you have tribu-
lation, but take courage;
I have overcome the world."

JOHN 16:33 NASB

While living in this world that you can touch
and see, you must remember that you are
also part of a world that can be known only
through faith. In the physical world
around you, you face disappointment
and struggle, yes. But as a citizen of
the kingdom of heaven, you are blessed
with a greater power—someone who
advocates for you. Jesus never claimed
you would be without struggle, but He
always reminds His followers of the
victory that is waiting.

Daily Walk

Just as you received Christ Jesus as
Lord, continue to live in him, rooted
and built up in him, strengthened
in the faith as you were taught, and
overflowing with thankfulness.

COLOSSIANS 2:6–7

Even though you don't always see progress
in your walk with God, you can be sure that
your roots are going down deep. Beneath the
soil, God tends your faith—the longer you
walk with Him, the deeper His hold on you.
You came to Him with nothing and simply
surrendered to His love. And that is all it
takes—just a willingness to keep walking
with Him and trusting that He's strengthen-
ing your roots beneath you.

Be very careful, then, how you live—
not as unwise but as wise.

EPHESIANS 5:15

As you walk with the Lord each day, you
will face many crossroads. God will open
the way before you, but He will not mandate
your steps. He's given you a free will with
which to choose the steps you take. He does
admonish you to choose wisely, though. The
safest way to do that is to keep your hand
in God's hand at all times. He will never let
you wander off the path. Reach out to Him
and He'll be there.

Decisions

The human mind plans the way,
but the Lord directs the steps.

PROVERBS 16:9 NRSV

It's always good to have a plan. It's also good to acknowledge that plans change—and sometimes those detours actually lead us to a better way. Make your lists, set your priorities, perfect your agendas, and work them well. But in the midst of it all, remember to surrender them to God. Then sit back and watch what your willing and prepared heart can do in the light of His direction.

"Who has known the mind of the Lord
that he may instruct him?"
But we have the mind of Christ.

1 CORINTHIANS 2:16

When you receive Christ, you are regenerated spiritually and given a renewed way of thinking. The Spirit of God makes His home in you. You have the mind of Christ. Given all that, shouldn't this life be easy? Shouldn't you always know what to do? Not necessarily. You still have your own nature and will, but you also have a resource to turn to. As you quiet yourself and learn to hear the mind of Christ within you, the way does become clearer.

Desires

The desires of the diligent
are fully satisfied.

PROVERBS 13:4

It's a fact of life that you don't always get
what you want. You've been learning that
lesson since you were two and the floor
wasn't too far away to stage a tantrum.
But now that you are pretty far from the
floor, you have to remember that there's
a difference between having everything
you want and being satisfied. God doesn't
promise to fulfill your every craving, but if
you live life in relationship to Him, you will
be satisfied—fully satisfied.

> Delight yourself in the Lord
> and he will give you the desires
> of your heart.
>
> PSALM 37:4

What does your heart desire? How much of your mental space does that desire occupy? The teachings of the Bible address the irony of the desires of our hearts. When we focus our attention on God, good things come to us. Even those things we want the most. It's easy to think you should do the opposite— fight for what you want. The twist in the plot is that when you delight in God, your heart's desires are most easily met.

Determination

As for you, be strong and do not give up, for your work will be rewarded.

2 CHRONICLES 15:7

What is it that's threatening to make you lose your resolve and give up? Maybe it's exhaustion or discouragement. It might be niggling questions like, "Is this worth it? Is anyone going to notice?" The Bible promises over and over again that your determination will be rewarded. God sees even if no one else does. He understands the process and the difficulty. He will be waiting at the finish line, and your efforts in this life will be well worth it.

Let us hold fast the confession
of our hope without wavering,
for He who promised is faithful.

HEBREWS 10:23 NKJV

There's not a lot of faithfulness around these days. People make promises, but circumstances change. Life twists and turns. But God is faithful. The promises He's made, He'll keep. You don't always know how and when, and sometimes life can mislead you into thinking your hope is lost. But if you are determined to hold on, the fog will eventually clear and your course will become clear. God's counting on you to stay the course and never give up.

Devotion

Love the LORD your God with all
your heart and with all your soul
and with all your strength.

DEUTERONOMY 6:5

We talk about loving someone from the heart, but loving someone actually takes all of us. We don't just love God with our hearts. We love him with our hearts, our souls, and our strength—we love him with our whole selves. That's the kind of love He wants from you. You can lose your own self-focus in giving that kind of whole-self devotion, and losing your self-focus is what a surrendered life is all about.

Guard my life,
for I am devoted to you.
You are my God;
save your servant who trusts in you.

PSALM 86:2

Devotion to God comes with strings attached—or maybe it would be better to say promises. When you give yourself completely to God, you become an heir to eternal life, and a child of His kingdom. Success is guaranteed in whatever you do because you are carrying out His will. Give Him every room in your heart. Open every door wide and invite Him in. When He comes, He brings with Him peace, joy, love, and much more.

Encouragement

You hear, O LORD, the desire of
the afflicted; you encourage them,
and you listen to their cry.

PSALM 10:17

It's easy to feel unheard in this life. Even
those closest to you may sometimes fail to
listen. But God hears. He's never too tired,
too busy, too distracted. You don't need an
appointment. He's always listening, always
encouraging. So cry out to Him. Share
everything with Him—those things that
cause you pain, those things that bring you
joy. Let Him in on your secrets and
your hopes. He will never fail you.

Think of ways to encourage one
another to outbursts of love
and good deeds.

HEBREWS 10:24 NLT

The great thing about Christian community is that we inspire each other in this
Christian walk. Haven't you caught someone
red-handed in some kind of faithful act,
and felt inspired? And who knows how
many times your faith has been spotted and
someone made a better choice "next time"
because they saw the choice you made.
That's the wonder of rubbing elbows in
the fray together. Faith alone strengthens
you. But faith together inspires more faith!

Eternal Life

Jesus said, "God so loved the world
that he gave his one and only Son,
that whoever believes in him shall
not perish but have eternal life."

JOHN 3:16

Life here on earth is fleeting. One day we
are sitting on the floor playing with our
favorite dolls, and then we find ourselves
a grown-up woman dealing with grown-up
issues. In what seems like a moment, we
notice gray hair and wrinkles tickling the
borders of our youthful faces. Life happens,
and that's why God created a way for us to
live on, free from time and age. Through His
Son, He bought eternal life for you. What
greater gift could there be?

Jesus said, "My sheep listen to my
voice; I know them, and they follow
me. I give them eternal life, and they
will never die, and no one can
steal them out of my hand."

JOHN 10:27–28 NCV

In eternity, we will have no need of protection. All will be well as we occupy the
heavenly kingdom. But here on earth, there
are many hazards. God has not left your
eternal life to chance. He purchased it for
you with the sacrifice of His own Son. Then,
He Himself watches over you so that nothing and no one can keep you from reaching
your destination. The life God has given you
is not up for the taking. It is sealed by His
promise.

Example

Be an example to the believers with
your words, your actions, your love,
your faith, and your pure life.

1 TIMOTHY 4:12 NCV

Setting an example for others can seem like
a heavy weight—always having to watch your
words and your actions. Being good on your
own is a simple impossibility. There's only
one way that you can live worthy to represent
God. That is by letting Him live through you.
When your self-interest crowds to the fore-
front, surrender yourself to Him. Soon
you will find yourself demonstrating
for others that it's possible to live
a pure and godly life.

Provide people with a glimpse of
good living and of the living God.

Have you ever heard someone say, "Your
actions are talking so loud that I can't hear
what you're saying!" It's true—people pay
much more attention to what you do than
what you say. That's why the way you
live as a child of God is crucial. Those
who would dismiss you as a religious
fanatic when you try to talk to them
about your relationship with your
Creator will be unable to ignore your
exemplary life. Let them see Jesus
in you.

Expectations

In the morning, O LORD, you hear my
voice; in the morning I lay my requests
before you and wait in expectation.

PSALM 5:3

It takes a lot of faith to hope. Even more to
expect. But you can do both when it comes to
your faith and your prayers. It's not that you
will always pray for a specific thing and get
it, like placing a catalog order online (not
that that always works out either). But what
you can expect, when you lay your concerns
before God, is that He will answer. Your
prayers do not fall on disregarding ears. You
can count on that.

Jesus said, "Be ready all the time.
For I, the Messiah,
will come when least expected."
LUKE 12:40 TLB

Jesus promised His return, and He asked that His followers watch for Him. He hasn't told us when—only that it will be when the world least expects Him. Only those who are sensitive to His Holy Spirit will recognize the times and the seasons. He expects you to live with the certainty that He will return soon, and to live your life accordingly. What a glorious day that will be. Look for it! Expect it!

Faith

Keep alert, stand firm in your faith,
be courageous, be strong.
Let all that you do be done in love.

1 CORINTHIANS 16:13–14 NRSV

Faith is not something you commit to
once then don't think about again. Instead
it's something that alerts you every day to
possibilities and opportunities. God has
called you to live a life of vibrant faith,
open to His direction, keeping your eyes
on Him. Day by day you will see His faithfulness and your faith will grow. Soon
you will stop worrying about what
is around the next corner. You'll
know with certainty that the two
of you can handle any eventuality.

We live by faith, not by sight.

2 CORINTHIANS 5:7

You've probably heard it before—seeing is
not believing; believing is seeing. It's more
than a twist on a phrase. Your faith opens
you up to a new awareness of life around
you. It enables you to see more from God's
point of view. It reminds you that life
is not just about the everyday realities
but also mystery and possibilities. When
you believe, you live according to a whole
other reality with sights and sounds
unimaginable to faithless eyes.

Faithfulness

The faithful will abound with blessings.

PROVERBS 28:20 NRSV

We've all had tasks that looked easy at the onset, but later threatened to scuttle our resolve. We wonder if it's worth it to hang on. But when we do, we find that the reward of the task accomplished is even sweeter. Are you wondering if you can finish the task God has assigned to you? Don't give up. Your faithfulness to God's purposes holds the promise of great reward. Ask God to help you faithfully carry on until the job is done.

Your love, O Lord,
reaches to the heavens,
your faithfulness to the skies.

PSALM 36:5

God won't abandon you. He won't walk
away. His faithfulness reaches farther than
you can see or even imagine. It's difficult
to take in that kind of faithfulness when
you live in a world full of disappointments.
But if you can get quiet enough inside to
sense God's never-changing presence and
His steadfast commitment to you, you can
survive the disappointments of this life so
much more bravely. His faithfulness never
fails!

Family

All thy children shall be taught
of the LORD; and great shall be
the peace of thy children.

ISAIAH 54:13 KJV

There's no heritage like the knowledge
of God's love. There's no inheritance as
empowering. As you live your life of faith
before your family, it's like stocking a vault
that will bless everyone. And it's never too
late to begin. As you live authentically before
God, you leave a blueprint for those who
are watching. That example can last
for generations, beyond your view,
more influential than you can
fathom.

A wise woman strengthens her family.

PROVERBS 14:1 NCV

The influence of a woman on her family is phenomenal—for good and for bad. Sadly, some women weaken their families through selfishness, ambition, and carelessness. The vigilant, wise, and godly woman holds her family together, makes sacrifices to ensure its stability, and entreats God's blessing with her prayers. You can be that kind of woman—the kind that builds up and strengthens. Ask God to help you. He will show you how.

Feelings

We can be sure when we say,
"I will not be afraid, because
the Lord is my helper."

HEBREWS 13:6 NCV

Women are complex beings. Our
emotions are our greatest strength, but
they can also be the most unstable aspect of
our character. How do you respond to the
pressures and pleasures around you each
day? Do you find yourself too emotional?
God doesn't want to stifle your emotions—
they allow you to feel His love, His compassion, His joy. Instead, He wants to help you
harness them and use them for His kingdom.
Will you let Him?

> When times are good, be happy;
> but when times are bad, consider:
> God has made the one
> as well as the other.

ECCLESIASTES 7:14

You may tend to think of God gratefully in the good times and ask for His help in the bad. But sometimes you have to consider that God brings good out of both. No matter what your feelings tell you, you can trust Him to work out His purpose in you at all times. He isn't bound by your feelings. He is bound by His Word. You should not be bound by your feelings either but by His promises!

Fellowship

If we are living in the light of
God's presence, just as Christ does,
then we have wonderful fellowship
and joy with each other.

1 JOHN 1:7 TLB

Living in close relationship with God empowers you to connect with people meaningfully. As you grow toward Him, you will find yourself growing in your relationships with others, as well. It's the result of having the same heavenly Father, living in the same kingdom, and sharing the same destination—heaven. Enjoy the great spiritual family God has placed you in. It's the family of faith. Be there for them and let them be there for you. It's what God intended.

All of you should be in agreement,
understanding each other,
loving each other as family,
being kind and humble.

1 PETER 3:8 NCV

The family of God is in many respects
like your natural family. You love them profoundly, but very often they can make you
throw up your hands in frustration.
Just like you, they all have those little
areas where they are still growing and
learning and becoming better people.
When conflicts come, don't turn and
run! It's important to work it out and
see it through—for your Father's sake.

Finances

Wealth hastily gotten will dwindle,
but those who gather little
by little will increase it.

PROVERBS 13:11 NRSV

In a world where people win lotteries and
game shows to suddenly come into a lot of
cash, it's easy to wonder if it's worth it to put
that little bit into savings each paycheck.
The Bible says a lot about money, though,
and affirms that it is the wise person who
builds that nest egg as they can, a little at a
time along the way. Besides the investment,
that bit you put away, no matter how small,
is a vote for your future.

My God will meet all your needs
according to his glorious
riches in Christ Jesus.

PHILIPPIANS 4:19

It may seem strange to learn that God cares
about money. While He isn't subject to it,
He knows that you are—while you live in
this world at least. The Bible provides good
advice about staying out of debt, saving all
you can, being generous with others, and
giving to the support of God's work. These
habits put you in line for God's blessings.
He describes them as "running over" and
invites you to test Him and see.

Forgiveness

I forgive you all that you have done,
says the Lord God.

EZEKIEL 16:63 NRSV

You are forgiven. No matter what you've done. No matter how or when or what— God's forgiveness is waiting for you. The moment you acknowledge your sin and ask to be forgiven, it's done. Strangely, that may be difficult for you to accept. You may feel you must make your own atonement. But it's a feat you will never accomplish. Only God's perfect Son was able to do the job. Abandon your pride and receive His forgiveness. Don't wait another moment.

Bear with one another and,
if anyone has a complaint against
another, forgive each other;
just as the Lord has forgiven you,
so you also must forgive.

COLOSSIANS 3:13 NRSV

If you've ever tried to forgive another person, even a close friend or family member, you know how difficult that can be. Everything in you wants to cling to the hurt and publish the offense. God invites you to forgive out of gratitude for what He's done for you. He has forgiven you—freely and completely. Remember that no one could hurt you as much as your sin has hurt your heavenly Father. When you look at it that way, forgiveness becomes a privilege.

Freedom

The LORD sets prisoners free.
PSALM 146:7

Some women run from God, thinking He will ask them to surrender their freedom and lock them down to some religious regimen. In reality, just the opposite is true. We are all already in bondage to our unwashed thoughts and behaviors and our sinful nature. Before you can flourish in God's kingdom, He has to remove your bonds. Fortunately, your heavenly Father is in the chain-breaking business. Ask Him to set you free.

The Lord is the Spirit,
and where the Spirit of the Lord is,
there is freedom.

2 Corinthians 3:17

Wherever the Spirit of God goes, freedom follows. If His Spirit dwells in you, you will experience more freedom than you have ever known. You will no longer be inhibited by selfishness and resentment. You will be free to do what you were created to do—live in right relationship with your Creator. Don't struggle to free yourself. You haven't the power or the strength. Invite God's Holy Spirit to come inside your heart and free you in the process.

Fresh Start

I will give you a new heart and
put a new spirit within you.

EZEKIEL 36:26 NKJV

Some of the most surprising news about
God's presence is that He does more than
fix you up the best He can and send you on
your way—somehow He makes you brand-
new. His offer of new life is one of the few
truly fresh starts you can experience. Sure,
He doesn't delete the consequences that still
have to be battled through—but He does have
the power to change your heart and help
you manage those consequences.

Ask Him to make you new!

You have begun to live the new life,
in which you are being made new
and are becoming like the
One who made you.

COLOSSIANS 3:10 NCV

God's work in your life doesn't simply
make you a better person; it makes you more
like Him! That's really true of any loving
relationship—the more you focus on
another person and interact with him
or her, the more you pick up that person's
habits and interests. In the same way—
but even more because of the work of the
Spirit—as you focus on God and interact
with Him, His nature is recovered in
your life.

Friendship

A friend loves at all times.
He is there to help
when trouble comes.

PROVERBS 17:17 NIrV

Tough times reveal real friends. Partly that is true because real friends are the ones that stick around when things are troublesome and uncomfortable and not-at-all-fun. But also it is true because when you are at your worst or weakest, you can only bear to be witnessed by real friends—those who already know you inside and out and accept you just the way you are. Ask God to give you that kind of friend.

Some friends play at friendship
but a true friend sticks closer
than one's nearest kin.

PROVERBS 18:24 NRSV

It's nice to have acquaintances. But somewhere within us, we crave authentic friendships that provide a connection as strong as that of our biological families. Do you have friendships that reach to this level? If not, ask God to help you find the ones that you can go deeper with. Then keep your eyes and ears open. Reach out to others, and let God do the rest. He won't disappoint you.

Fruitfulness

Jesus said, "Abide in me as I abide
in you. Just as the branch cannot
bear fruit by itself unless it abides
in the vine, neither can you
unless you abide in me."

JOHN 15:4 NRSV

You may think you aren't accomplishing
anything in your life. Perhaps you work at
a dead-end job or a disability has left you
feeling useless and alone. No matter what
your circumstances, God has a plan for you,
and that plan is not out of reach. As long as
you are looking to Him, your life will
be fruitful and fulfilling. That's His
will, His promise, and His plan.

Jesus said, "You did not choose me, but I chose you and appointed you to go and bear fruit—fruit that will last."

JOHN 15:16

Have you looked at yourself and thought, *God could never use me.* You've just decided that you aren't worthy to go out in His name, to speak on His behalf, to carry His message, to fulfill His plan. If it were up to you, you wouldn't appoint yourself to do anything. But it isn't up to you. God does the choosing, and He wants to use you. He's given you a job to do. Open your heart and mind to Him, and much fruit will follow.

Future

I know the plans I have for you,
says the Lord, plans for your
welfare and not for harm,
to give you a future with hope.

JEREMIAH 29:11 NRSV

Your age doesn't matter. Your looks
don't matter. Your circumstances don't
matter. For every individual, every life, God
has a plan for the future. Even if you are
reading this book from a hospital bed from
which you never expect to leave, God has
given you a future. Don't drop out of life for
any reason. With Him, your best days are
yet to come—better than you can think or
imagine.

Good people can look forward
to a bright future.

PROVERBS 13:9 NCV

When your life is hid in the goodness of God, your possibilities are limitless. Your future is more than bright—it's dazzling. If you are at the beginning of your walk with God, you are a fortunate woman. The road ahead may not be easy, but it will be the greatest adventure, the greatest race you've ever attempted. And best of all, the destination is certain. Throw yourself unreservedly into the work that God has called you to. Take hold of your future with both hands.

Gentleness

Take my yoke upon you and learn from
me, for I am gentle and humble in heart,
and you will find rest for your souls.

MATTHEW 11:29

God could blast you for your sinfulness.
He could reprimand you every time you
stumble and chastise you for every mistake
you make. He will correct you, of course.
How else can He keep you on the right path?
But God's correction is consistently gentle.
No throwing of lightning bolts and crashing
thunderclaps, just a still small voice
inside your heart. He will not
make an excuse for your sin,
but He will quietly and gently
call you to repentance.

Let your gentleness be evident to all.
The Lord is near.

PHILIPPIANS 4:5

The Bible says that the strong woman is also gentle—two words that might seem contradictory. But they aren't. The strong woman chooses how she will respond to others. She chooses to deal with them gently—because she can. She is in control of her emotions, her words, and her actions. Anger, hostility—both represent the easy way out. But gentleness requires strength. God wants to see you become a strong, gentle woman for Him.

Goodness

When wisdom enters your heart, and
knowledge is pleasant to your soul. . .
you may walk in the way of goodness.

PROVERBS 2:10, 20 NKJV

When you were a little girl, your parents
may have said, "Run along now and be a
good little girl." They meant only the best,
but growing up, many women received a
negative message. They relate goodness to
being dismissed or not being taken seriously.
Others become obsessed with meeting an
unrealistic standard of goodness. Really no
one is good but God. Goodness will come as
you walk in relationship with Him.

As we have opportunity,
let us do good to all people,
especially to those who belong
to the family of believers.

GALATIANS 6:10

Good deeds are an expression of the
goodness or "God-ness" that resides within
you. They should come easily, naturally.
As you feel God's presence within and see
Him moving in your affairs, as you feel your
heart flooding with gratitude for what He
has done for you, reach out to others. Let
them feel the overflow of God's goodness to
you. Good deeds aren't something you force
yourself to do. They are the joyous privilege
of the child of God.

Grace

By the grace of God I am what I am,
and his grace to me was not
without effect. No, I worked harder than
all of them—yet not I, but
the grace of God that was with me.

1 CORINTHIANS 15:10

Grace is often defined as God's unmerited favor. It means that His love for us, His care, and His concern are all free gifts—we haven't earned them. What a wonderful thing to be loved and accepted—just because! In God's eyes, you are already pretty enough, smart enough, good enough to receive His best. He loves you for yourself. He wants you to become all you were created to be, but your relationship with Him doesn't hinge on it. What a wonderful word "grace" is!

[God] gives grace to the humble.

PROVERBS 3:34

For many people, it's difficult to receive
what they don't feel they have earned.
Whether it's a sense of independence or
pride, such an attitude will rob you of the
best this life has to offer. You must be
able to receive God's love, even when
you don't feel lovable, and God's goodness, even when you don't feel deserving.
God has freely given you everything—His
kingdom! Don't stand on the sidelines
whispering, "I'm not worthy." Humble
yourself and receive.

Guidance

Your ears shall hear a word behind you, saying, "This is the way, walk in it," whenever you turn to the right hand or whenever you turn to the left.

ISAIAH 30:21 NKJV

When we need answers, we often say we are "seeking God." And yet, we need not seek Him since He is ever near. Nor are we seeking answers from God, for He has already given us the answers we need. Instead, we are seeking to hear those answers, to tune out the busy thoughts and preconceived notions we carry with us. If you need answers, ask God to help you listen and discern, to open your ears to hear His voice that was there all along.

> I will instruct you and teach you
> in the way you should go;
> I will guide you with My eye.
>
> PSALM 32:8 NKJV

Have you been asking God for guidance, but the way before you is still unclear? It could be that you're expecting a full-blown road map—and God rarely answers that way. Instead, He gives the first step, and when you have taken that step, He reveals the next. That's how He encourages your faith and keeps you close to the path. It's enough really to know that He sees the path ahead. Trust Him!

Happiness

A happy heart makes the face cheerful,
but heartache crushes the spirit.

PROVERBS 15:13

Happiness is elusive in this life. Because it's an emotion—like sadness and anger—it comes and goes with the circumstances. Joy is different. It's the permanent condition of the heart that is right with God. It isn't based on circumstances, but rather the known outcome—eternity with God. Forget about the pursuit of happiness and embrace joy. It will not fail you even in your darkest days and most trying hours. Rejoice!

May the righteous be glad
and rejoice before God;
may they be happy and joyful.

PSALM 68:3

Many women believe that happiness is a result of success. "When I find the right person to marry, I'll be happy." "When I achieve my career goals. . ." "When I can afford the home I really want. . ." The truth is that real happiness—deep inner joy—is the result of living in right relationship with God rather than the trappings of success. Regardless of what you may be facing—good and bad—be happy knowing you are pleasing your heavenly Father.

Help

God is our refuge and strength,
an ever-present help in trouble.

PSALM 46:1

Have you ever gone through a trial or heartache so painful that you couldn't even put it into words? It felt like a long, piercing scream was ripping you apart inside. Any number of things could cause such suffering—loss, divorce, betrayal, sickness. If you find yourself in such a place in your life, reach out to the Lord. He understands suffering at its deepest level. He knows how to comfort you. All you have to do is ask.

Our soul waits for the LORD;
He is our help and our shield.

PSALM 33:20 NKJV

Who do you turn to when trouble comes
your way? You're blessed if you have faithful friends and loved ones here on earth.
But whether you have such support in your
life or not, God has promised you will never
face adversity alone. Again and again in the
Bible, He declares His desire to help you.
Even when no one else is there—He will be.
And He has limitless resources. No matter
what your need, call on Him.

Hope

The Lord is good to those who hope
in him, to those who seek him.

LAMENTATIONS 3:25 NCV

Hope is amazing. It can grow and thrive
even in the bleakest circumstances. A
prisoner of war suffers brutal abuse at the
hands of his captors, but they cannot break
his spirit or rob him of the hope that one day
he will be free again. It's hope that keeps us
moving forward, always looking for a better
day. Hope is God's gift. Thank Him for it
by placing your hope in Him. He is
profoundly faithful.

Why are you downcast, O my soul?
Why so disturbed within me?
Put your hope in God, for I will yet
praise him, My Savior and my God.

PSALM 42:5–6

People hope in many things—money, possessions, other people, power, fame, and status, even their own strength. None of those things have the power to sustain hope. But God does. Money and possessions can be gone in a moment, but He will never change. People will fail you, but He will never let you down. Power, fame, and status are remarkably fragile. Even your own strength will one day be gone. But God will still be by your side. Place your hope in Him.

Hospitality

Do not forget to do good
and to share with others,
for with such sacrifices God is pleased.

HEBREWS 13:16

The true meaning of hospitality is opening up your heart to others, making them feel at home in your presence. That means you can be hospitable anywhere you are. It doesn't require a fancy house or a gourmet meal. When you reach out to someone else with love and acceptance, you have shown that person hospitality. Look around you. Ask God to show you those people whom you can minister to just by opening your heart.

Do not neglect to show hospitality
to strangers, for by this some have
entertained angels without knowing it.

HEBREWS 13:2 NASB

It's easy enough to show hospitality to
your family and friends, but God asks that
you reach out to strangers, as well. That
takes courage. But God is pleased when
you look past your own shyness and hesita-
tion to touch the life of a person you don't
know. Instead of focusing on how it makes
you feel, think about how it could affect a
stranger—alone in a crowd. Your hospitality
has the power to change a life for eternity.

Humility

With humility comes wisdom.

PROVERBS 11:2 NLT

The Bible says that Jesus is the only begotten Son of God, ruling and reigning with His Father from their heavenly throne room. And yet, He did the unthinkable. He chose to be born as a baby, live as one of us, and then suffer reproach and abuse, finally death. He humbled Himself and allowed Himself to be placed on the cross—for you. His humility accomplished the plan of salvation. Imagine what your humble obedience to His will can accomplish.

> By humility and the fear of the LORD
> are riches, and honour, and life.
>
> PROVERBS 22:4 KJV

If you think being humble will make you a doormat for others to walk on and take advantage of, you couldn't be more wrong. Many associate humility with weakness, but it is more closely defined as strength. It takes no special effort to behave proudly. Pride comes naturally to human beings. But humility—that's not so easy. It means making a choice to do the difficult thing, the God thing. Submit yourself to God and reap the benefits of humility.

Integrity

I know, my God, that you test the heart
and are pleased with integrity.
All these things have I given willingly
and with honest intent.

1 CHRONICLES 29:17

Do you have a secret, something you are keeping hidden deep within, something that causes you to live in shame? You shouldn't think that you are keeping anything from God. He sees your heart. He knows all about you. And He wants to free you from the burden you are carrying. Confess your secret sins to Him—those you've committed and those committed against you. He will wash your heart clean. Then He will praise you as you live honestly and openly before Him.

> Whoever walks in integrity
> walks securely.
>
> PROVERBS 10:9 NRSV

Choosing to do the right thing in a situation
may be difficult, even painful. It could mean
the loss of income, a broken relationship, or
an embarrassing confrontation. But whatever it takes, keeping your integrity is vitally
important. When you do what is right, you
preserve your soul. You'll make mistakes—no
doubt about that—but God is there to forgive
you and help you stay on track in the future.
When you choose integrity, you choose the
Lord.

Justice

Don't insist on getting even; that's not
for you to do. "I'll do the judging,"
says God. "I'll take care of it."

Many times when we are mistreated,
we respond with vengeful thoughts and
actions, forgetting that we look to a higher
court—the authority of God. It isn't easy to
lay down your offense, especially when your
heart is aching for justice, but when you do,
God is able to act on your behalf. Seeking
revenge keeps you in a cycle of reciprocal
hurt. Laying your grievance before
God's high court frees you to move
on. Trust God's pure justice and
let Him fight your battles.

The LORD loves the just and
will not forsake his faithful ones.
They will be protected forever.

PSALM 37:28

Often we cry for justice when we have been
wronged, but not when we have wronged
others. God wants us to care about both—
because He does. Be sure that in all your
transactions you require a high standard of fairness from yourself. Ask God to
point out your blind spots so that your heart
might remain pure before Him. When you
mess up, be quick to make things right.
God will be watching—and applauding.

Kindness

When the kindness and love of God
our Savior appeared, he saved us,
not because of righteous things we
had done, but because of his mercy.

TITUS 3:4–5

Do you find it easy to offer kindness to those you feel deserve it—but not to those who don't? That's a normal human response. But when you begin to understand the fullness of God's kindness to you personally, you're apt to see things in a different light. You weren't deserving or even grateful, and yet He was kind to you. He held nothing back. Being kind to those who don't deserve it is a powerful way to demonstrate your likeness to your heavenly Father.

> Who can find a virtuous woman?
> for her price is far above rubies. . . .
> She openeth her mouth with wisdom;
> and in her tongue is the
> law of kindness.

PROVERBS 31:10, 26 KJV

Kindness is often misunderstood. It doesn't mean stepping back and letting others dictate to you. And it doesn't mean coddling and indulging others. It means being gentle, friendly, benevolent, and generous with another person, especially when there is no expectation of receiving anything from that person in return. You won't have to go looking for opportunities to be kind, they will appear on their own dozens of times a day. Be like your heavenly Father—be kind!

Leadership

Jesus said, "The greatest among you must become like the youngest, and the leader like one who serves."

LUKE 22:26 NRSV

Not everyone is called to be a leader, but if you feel God's call and sense you have been given the attributes you need to lead others, you are right to step out from the crowd and make it known. Just know that leadership in God's kingdom is a position of service. Like Moses and King David and Paul the apostle, God will humble you before He uses you. But if you're willing and obedient, He may use you to change the world.

Be ye followers of me,
even as I also am of Christ.

1 CORINTHIANS 11:1 KJV

In order to be a good leader in God's
kingdom, you must be a good follower—not
of others, but of God. You aren't charged
with setting the pace or cutting the path
before you, but of keeping your eyes
on the Lord and following His every
move. That means you must know the
principles He's laid out in the scriptures
and live in close and constant relationship with God. It's a big responsibility
to lead others, and a great privilege.

Learning

Let the wise listen
and add to their learning.

PROVERBS 1:5

Being a Christian is all about being a student in the things of God. What a wonderful blessing! Each day you are charged with getting to know your heavenly Father better and becoming more like Him. That will sometimes be painful as you discard old thought patterns and behaviors in favor of new ones, but it will always be productive, transforming you into the person God created you to be. Stay close to Him, listen, and learn all you can.

> Teach the righteous and
> they will gain in learning.
>
> PROVERBS 9:9 NRSV

The number-one characteristic of the unrighteous is their inability to learn. They make the same mistakes over and over, never recognizing their error or understanding that they have been given the power to change. You have seen the error of your ways and turned to God. Now continue to learn, continue to change, and continue to grow in the image of your heavenly Father. He is proud of your progress in righteousness.

Life

The way you tell me to live is always right; help me understand it so I can live to the fullest.

PSALM 119:144 MSG

God has given us guidelines to live by—principles laid out in amazing detail in the Bible. Some say His rules are simply designed to bolster His ego. That's the same lie the devil told Eve when He tempted her to disobey God in the Garden of Eden. "He's just trying to keep you from having something good," he taunted. Like any good parent, God has given us rules to ensure our safety and success. Living His way is always for your best.

Jesus said, "I have come that they may have life, and have it to the full."

JOHN 10:10

A baby spends nine months in its mother's womb becoming the person God has created it to be. In comparison to its life lived outside the womb, this preparation time is amazingly short. In the same way, our lives here on earth are relatively brief and intended as a time to grow and prepare for eternity with God. You are being groomed for eternal life. That will truly be living to the fullest measure.

Loneliness

I am convinced that. . .neither
the present nor the future, nor any
powers, neither height nor depth, nor
anything else in all creation, will be
able to separate us from the love of
God that is in Christ Jesus our Lord.

ROMANS 8:38–39

You don't have to be alone to feel lonely. It's
all about how you are connecting with those
around you. Perhaps you are in a place in your
life where you feel no one understands you and
no one cares. This time in your life probably
won't last long. You will make connections
and the loneliness will pass, but until it does,
remember that God has promised to always be
there for you—to listen, to comfort, to encourage. He's as close as your prayer.

God sets the lonely in families,
he leads forth the prisoners
with singing.

PSALM 68:6

It isn't God's will for you to feel alone or lonely. He has gone to great lengths to include you in His family and surround you with spiritual brothers and sisters. Open your heart and let God help you make connections with His people. You will find that Christian fellowship goes deeper than any relationships you have had. It has permanence and variety. God wants to send your loneliness packing. Let Him set you squarely in His family.

Love

From everlasting to everlasting the
LORD's love is with those who fear him,
and his righteousness with their
children's children.

PSALM 103:17

God loves you! It's not complicated or
conditional—it's just a fact! Our human
understanding can't comprehend the reason
why, only that it's true. As much as you
might want to explain it, dissect it, reason
it out, you just can't. Instead of wrapping
yourself in questions, wrap yourself in His
love. Luxuriate in it just as you would
a magnificent fur coat. God has
spared no expense. He has given
you the very best He has to offer.

"A new command I give you: Love one another. As I have loved you, so you must love one another. By this all men will know that you are my disciples, if you love one another."

JOHN 13:34–35

God loves you relentlessly, completely, and in spite of your flaws and shortcomings. His greatest desire is for you to love in the same way. He asks you first of all to love Him in return and then to love others. When you love you show that you are His child; you demonstrate who you are and what you're made of. That pleases your heavenly Father more than any great work you might do on His behalf. Live to please Him by loving others.

Marriage

Let marriage be held in honor by all.

HEBREWS 13:4 NRSV

Since God placed the first man and woman in the Garden of Eden, He has endorsed and blessed marriage. Except for those who have been set apart—like the apostle Paul—for singleness, God uses marriage as a tool to purify us. Through it He teaches lessons on faithfulness, trust, love, humility, service, gentleness, and much more. It is His refining fire. All the more reason to set your heart to live and grow within the boundaries of this holy union.

> Your Maker is your husband—
> the LORD Almighty is his name.
>
> ISAIAH 54:5

Women find themselves single all the time. Some are single by their own choice or as part of God's plan for their lives. Others may be divorced or widowed. If you are single for whatever reason, you may be surprised to learn that you are in a highly favored position. The Lord says that He is the one who will provide for you and defend you. You can look to Him for love and companionship. He's more faithful and wise than any human husband.

Nature

God's glory is on tour in the skies,
God-craft on exhibit
across the horizon.

PSALM 19:1 MSG

Look outside right now; better yet, go outside. Daytime or nighttime, it doesn't matter. Just look around you. If you live in a concrete jungle, look up at the sky. Imagine for a moment the immensity of God's creation, the grandeur of it. And yet, He calls mankind His most splendid creation—all the rest was called into being only to benefit His human creation. God values you above all else. Look up at the sky and consider that.

Jesus said, "Walk out into the fields
and look at the wildflowers."

MATTHEW 6:28 MSG

Our God cares about details. You see it
throughout His creation. Every species
unique and every creature unique within its
species. Human beings, created in His image and yet each one of a kind. Flowers and trees awash with color and
refinement, even those growing along
the highway, sown as it were by the wind.
When you wonder if God is interested
in the details of your life, consider the
evidence demonstrated in nature. He
cares about everything—no matter how
inconsequential.

Patience

Patience is better than strength.
PROVERBS 16:32 NCV

Our electronic world does not encourage patience. Internet providers tout newer, faster technologies. What used to take days, even weeks, can now be done in minutes. Not everything can be rushed, though. God still does things in His own way and His own timing. He won't be bullied or hurried. He wants to strengthen and test your faith. When you feel impatient waiting for God to move on your behalf, resolve to trust Him. Surrender yourself to Him. You can be sure that He knows best.

Be still before the Lord,
and wait patiently for him.

PSALM 37:7 NRSV

Do you remember as a child waiting for
Christmas morning or to open your pres-
ents on your birthday? "Just wait. It will all
happen in due time," your mother would
say. God won't withhold from you just to be
cruel or make a point, but He does see the
big picture, and He knows the right when,
where, and how. So don't get anxious, just
wait. You will see what God has promised
you—all in due time.

Peace

You, Lord, give true peace
to those who depend on you,
because they trust you.

ISAIAH 26:3 NCV

Peace is to the kingdom of God what oxygen is to the atmosphere. Considering this truth, you may be wondering why you so often feel agitated and anxious. Think of it this way. Though oxygen permeates the air around us, we must breathe it into our lungs for it to do us any good. You must choose to let God rule in your heart. You must invite Him in. As you open your heart to Him, the peace will follow.

Let the peace of Christ rule in your
hearts, since as members of one body
you were called to peace.

COLOSSIANS 3:15

God often uses peace as a way of giving His
children guidance. When you are praying
about an important decision or life choice,
you should pay close attention to the
amount of peace you have concerning it.
In any case, you should not move when
your peace is replaced by a sense of anxiety
or unrest. Move back in the other direction
until the peace returns. You will never go
wrong as long as you follow the peace.

Power

[God] gives strength to the weary
and increases the power of the weak.

ISAIAH 40:29

In the time of Jesus, widows and orphans
were the most disadvantaged members of
society. They were essentially powerless
in a culture where women were not valued
except through their husbands. These dis-
enfranchised women are often mentioned
in the New Testament, however. Jesus made
it clear that they were to be treated kindly,
with respect, and taken care of. He raised
them from their less-than-nothing status to
full acceptance in the body of believers. You
are never powerless when you belong
to Him.

> [Be] strengthened with all power
> according to his glorious might
> so that you may have great
> endurance and patience.
>
> COLOSSIANS 1:11

There aren't enough hours in the day to do a woman's work. No wonder we often feel exhausted and unhappy. The Bible says that there is a remedy for our endless activity. He strengthens us, empowering us to push through and get our jobs done. Sometimes He does that by empowering us to say "no" when we should, rest when we should, and keep our lives balanced. Ask Him for a transfusion for your life.

Praise

Ye are a chosen generation,
a royal priesthood, an holy nation,
a peculiar people; that ye should shew
forth the praises of [God] who
hath called you out of darkness
into his marvellous light.

1 Peter 2:9 kjv

Your life is a song of praise that rises to God
your Father. He revels in your decision to take
His hand and step out of darkness into light.
It's what He has worked so hard to accomplish.
It's why He sent His Son, Jesus, to live and
die and rise again. You are His trophy, His
prize, the sure and certain reward of
His great sacrifice. Each time you say
yes to life, yes to love, yes to eternal
values, you are praising Him.

I will praise You, O Lord,
with my whole heart. . . . I will sing
praise to Your name, O Most High.

PSALM 9:1–2 NKJV

Your life is a form of praise, but your words
of praise are even more precious to your
heavenly Father. His Holy Spirit who lives
within you carries them straight to His
throne. Why are your praises so dear to
Him? Because, unlike His other creatures, your praises are not innate. They
are the free expression of your heart. You
chose Him when you could have chosen
so many others. Lift your voice to Him.
It brings Him great joy.

Prayer

Pray and ask God for everything
you need, always giving thanks.

PHILIPPIANS 4:6 NCV

Prayer is quite simply conversation with
God. What a joyous privilege we have to
be able to speak to Him—almighty God—
whenever we desire. How could you ever get
enough of those times with Him? Meet with
Him often to talk about your life. Tell Him
your troubles and leave your worries at His
feet. Confess your sins to Him and receive
His forgiveness. Tell Him how much you
love Him and how grateful you are to be His
daughter. He's always ready to listen.

> When you call upon me and come
> and pray to me, I will hear you. When
> you search for me, you will find me;
> if you seek me with all your heart.
>
> JEREMIAH 29:12–13 NRSV

Is there a great need in your life? Something you have struggled with and can't seem to find the answer for? God says to bring it to Him—not just once but again and again. Keep asking. Keep reminding Him of His promises. Like a child who campaigns for a new bike, never give up. Seek God and keep on seeking Him. He hears you each and every time, and He will reward your persistence and your patience after He proves your heart.

Presence of God

Blessed are those who have learned
to acclaim you, who walk in the light
of your presence, O Lord.

PSALM 89:15

Close your eyes and imagine yourself sitting on the beach, a warm breeze tickling your skin and the comforting sound of waves breaking on the shore. Or think of yourself in a garden, the sounds of songbirds and enchanting fragrances in every direction. Place yourself anywhere, but know that nothing can compare to being in the presence of God. The treasures of the universe are stored there, His love surrounds you, and peace flows like a beautiful river. Come and enjoy.

Jesus said, "Where two or three
come together in my name,
there am I with them."

MATTHEW 18:20

God loves to be where His people are.
His Holy Spirit dwells in each one of them,
but when believers come near each other,
something heavenly happens—not only
does He dwell in them, but He also
fills the distance between them. In
this atmosphere, the impossible becomes
possible and love becomes manifest. God
urges you to meet together with other
believers regularly. He knows what can
happen when you do.

Priorities

Fear God and keep his commandments,
for this is the whole duty of man.

ECCLESIASTES 12:13

God knows how busy your life is. As you
move from task to task, remember to hold
on to the golden cord that connects you
to Him. He's always there regardless, but
the cord reminds you that He is. It keeps
the conversation going between the two of
you, and His love, joy, and peace flowing
to you throughout your day. God should be
your first priority because it is through His
wisdom and strength that you accomplish
the others.

> Seek those things which are above, where Christ is, sitting at the right hand of God. Set your mind on things above, not on things on the earth.

COLOSSIANS 3:1–2 NKJV

Human beings can be hopelessly short-sighted. But the person who sees past today and plans for eternity has both the present and the future in mind. When you accepted Christ's sacrifice for you on the cross and asked God to forgive your sins, your future in heaven was sealed. But the Bible also talks about laying up treasure in heaven. Place your priorities on those things that are eternal rather than those things that are just for this world alone.

Protection

The Lord your God will lead you
and protect you on every side.

ISAIAH 52:12 GNT

We all have fears—fear of harm, fear of losing a child, fear of being alone, fear of failure. When your fears rise up and threaten to overcome you. When you feel sick in the pit of your stomach and your heart aches with anxiety—remember this. God is with you, every day, every hour, every moment. Focus on Him, really focus, and you will see that your fears are nothing more than speculation that is swept away in His presence.

The LORD watches over all
who love him.

PSALM 145:20

Like any loving parent, your heavenly
Father keeps you in His constant care,
never letting you out of His sight. You have
no reason to fear, for He is always with
you, ready to face whatever comes
your way. He will not fail you. In
some cases, He will warn you ahead of
time. In others, He will supernaturally
remove you from a dangerous situation.
And there will be times when He will
hold your hand as you walk through
fire. He is your God!

Provision

God will generously provide
all you need. Then you will always
have everything you need and plenty
left over to share with others.

2 CORINTHIANS 9:8 NLT

God has promised to take care of you, but
it doesn't stop there. He wants to provide for
you abundantly—so much that you can share
it with others. His provision isn't limited to
money. He is the provider of all you need. If
you need joy, He'll give it to you with enough
to share. If you need wisdom, it's there for
you, as well. Whatever you have on your
list—ask Him for it. Then trust Him.

Jesus said, "Your Father knows what you need before you ask him."

MATTHEW 6:8

God wants you to have everything you need for a great life. But sometimes we pray and things don't happen when we expect them to. You must trust that His timing is perfect. None of us live in a vacuum. Sometimes your request requires compliance on the part of other people, and they may not be prompt to respond. Don't give up. God will answer your prayer in the perfect way at the perfect time.

Relationships

Be devoted to one another
in brotherly love. Honor one
another above yourselves.

ROMANS 12:10

Jesus' ultimate sacrifice—laying down His
life so that all humanity could experience
eternal life—showed true devotion. His
willingness to go to the cross gave you the
opportunity to experience an intimacy with
God that was not available before. Likewise
you can honor others with the same love. That
strength and power of love resides within
you. God gave you the ability to show
His love to everyone you meet. Be
bold! Be courageous! Love like
Jesus does! It's in you!

Kinsfolk are born to share adversity.

PROVERBS 17:17 NRSV

Your family holds a powerful place in
your life. The same is true of your sisters
and brothers in the Lord. They know your
greatest strengths and most intimate
weaknesses—but with a different agenda.
The family of God is to build you up
in the area of your weakness and draw
from you in the area of your strengths.
Though often painful, this is a process
designed to make you strong and fruitful. There is great reward in enduring
the adversity of relationships.

Renewal

Create in me a pure heart, O God, and
renew a steadfast spirit within me.

PSALM 51:10

No two snowflakes are alike. No two sunsets are ever exactly the same. Your Creator delivers a masterpiece with every stroke of artistry He inspires. You are no different. With each touch of His hand, with every letter you read in His Word, He changes your heart from old to new—forming you in His image. You become more like Him each moment you spend with Him. Your Creator makes all things new—and He's continually shaping the perfect you!

> Though outwardly we are wasting
> away, yet inwardly we are being
> renewed day by day.
>
> 2 CORINTHIANS 4:16

Your relationship with God is alive. It's living and breathing and requires nourishment to survive. Much like tributaries pour into lakes and rivers, you give out of your spirit into all you do. When you give out, you can drain your reserves. God wants you full. Fill up as you renew your spirit and mind daily with His Word and in His presence. You're a life-giving river of living water. Fill up, pour out, and fill up again!

Respect

A kindhearted woman gains respect.
PROVERBS 11:16

As you grow in God, you begin to demonstrate His character and nature in your thoughts, attitudes, and behavior. Through you, His goodness becomes evident to others, and their respect for you increases. This will happen not because you demand it but because it is a natural response to God's glory. For the same reason, you must respect yourself—casting down thoughts of inferiority and unworthiness. Respect God's presence and work within you.

> Knowledge begins with
> respect for the Lord.
>
> PROVERBS 1:7 NCV

The Hebrews who walked across the Red Sea had such a reverence for God that they never said His name out loud. They had great respect for Him. Though your relationship with God is much different today, He still desires your respect. You are His child and He adores you. You are privileged to show Him your admiration. Give Him respect through praise, worship, and adoration. He wants to hear you—His precious child—say His name!

Responsibility

Whatever you do, work at it with all
your heart, as working for the Lord,
not for men, since you know that
you will receive an inheritance from
the Lord as a reward. It is the
Lord Christ you are serving.

COLOSSIANS 3:23–24

Sometimes it may feel like your hard work
goes unnoticed. Maybe you're tempted to slack
off like the other guy, telling yourself that no
one will ever know. God knows your heart. The
One that holds the future in His hands sees
your faithfulness. He has entrusted you with
much responsibility because He knows He
can count on you. He will reward you and will
bring you into a place of blessing. Expect it and
believe He'll do it. God applauds you!

There are different kinds of service,
but the same Lord.

1 CORINTHIANS 12:5

You may feel the weight of responsibilities
you have been given. God made your shoulders broad enough to carry all that has been
assigned to you. Embrace your responsibility knowing God has given you grace to
carry it—and when it seems too heavy, He's
always there to help you. He won't leave you
alone to do what He's asked you to do. He
won't let you fall under the weight. He won't
condemn you for stumbling under the load.
He's there for you!

Rest

The beloved of the Lord rests in
safety—the High God surrounds him
all day long—the beloved rests
between his shoulders.

DEUTERONOMY 33:12 NRSV

When you think of rest—you probably
think of a nap or picture yourself soaking
in a tub. While you need physical rest, God
wants your soul well rested and full of His
presence, as well. Read encouraging scriptures that build your faith. Spend time with
Him in prayer. You'll feel like you've had
a spiritual power nap. You'll come
away rested and strengthened in
your soul, safe from the assaults
of the day.

On the seventh day God. . .
rested from all his work.

GENESIS 2:2 NLT

Many women put in forty hours a week at
a full-time job and then come home to care
for the house and family. Don't forget to
take time-out for you. If God rested after
working all week, then it's important
to take care of yourself. The list of
things to do will wait. Press the pause
button and rest your mind, body, and
emotions. You're precious and valuable
to God and all of those who love you.
You're worth it. Take a moment and
relax.

Reward

You know that the Lord will reward
everyone for whatever good he does.

EPHESIANS 6:8

Have you ever received a reward for an
act of kindness? Maybe you returned a wallet
or found a lost pet. So often the goodness
of God goes unnoticed. He gives with open
hands never expecting anything in return
because His motivation is love. He loved you
enough to give up everything. You can give
something to God. Become the rewarder!
Let Him know that His grace and mercy have
not gone unnoticed. Reward Him with your
praise and thanksgiving.

The LORD recompense thy work,
and a full reward be given thee.

Perhaps you feel unappreciated for the things you do for others—the cooking, cleaning, a late night at the office. Just once a thank-you would be reward enough. Someone does take notice of all you do. Your heavenly Father is watching even when it seems no one notices. He's proud of you and appreciates all you do. You show the love and life of God to those around you. Take heart—God is your exceedingly great reward.

Righteousness

The work of righteousness shall be
peace; and the effect of righteousness
quietness and assurance for ever.

ISAIAH 32:17 KJV

What a comfort it is to know that God
has paid the price for all your mistakes and
declared you righteous based on the life
of His own flawless Son. When the enemy
comes to condemn you, the blood of Jesus
stands between you and anything the devil
accuses you of. Jesus paid the price and God
found you righteous—without blame. Rest
assured that God is on your side.
You've been cleared of any wrong-
doing by the Highest Court.
You're right in God's eyes.

The path of the righteous is like the first gleam of dawn, shining ever brighter till the full light of day.

PROVERBS 4:18

God knows where you're going. As you journey on the road toward God's purpose and plan for your life, the light of God's love grows brighter with each step, bringing you closer and closer to Him. The more you know Him, the more quickly you know His will and His ways and can more assuredly step out in faith toward His righteous cause. Your steps are sure because your path is well lit with the goodness of God. You're on the right path.

Sacrifice

The sacrifices of God are a broken
spirit; a broken and contrite heart,
O God, you will not despise.

PSALM 51:17

No matter where you've been, God loves
you. He doesn't care about your past, but
instead wants to give you an awesome future.
You were worth the ultimate sacrifice. God
gave all He had for you—at the highest cost.
He cherishes you more than anything. You
are the high prize that His Son, Jesus, was
willing to fight and die for in order to re-
store you to your heavenly Father. Give Him
your brokenness. It's a sacrifice you can
afford to make.

> I urge you. . .in view of God's mercy, to offer your bodies as living sacrifices, holy and pleasing to God— this is your spiritual act of worship.
>
> ROMANS 12:1

You are the greatest house ever built. The King of kings desired to take up residence in you. Just like you'd expect a palace to be well cared for, so you should take care of your own body. Choosing to live a pure and holy life brings honor and glory to Him. Your character and behavior testify of His residence much like the lawn of a palace speaks of the royal family and their stature. Rejoice! You are the temple of the most High God.

Salvation

[God] says, "In the time of my favor
I heard you, and in the day of salvation
I helped you." I tell you,
now is the time of God's favor,
now is the day of salvation.

2 CORINTHIANS 6:2

Jesus' death on the cross was God's plan
to bring you into heaven once your time on
earth is through. But God had much more in
mind than you might imagine. Jesus' death,
burial, and resurrection offer freedom from
any bondage you face. God doesn't want you to
miss a single blessing. Let Him save you
from worry, addiction, debt, sickness,
and emotional pain. Every promise
in the book belongs to you. Don't
wait to receive His great salvation.

> Once made perfect, [Christ] became the source of eternal salvation for all who obey him.
>
> HEBREWS 5:9

You are truly the perfect woman. Others may bring up your past or point out your mistakes, but God has made you perfect through Christ Jesus. Your old life is passed away and all things are new. You have a fresh start—a clean slate. God doesn't remember the old you. Every sin has been forgotten in His mind. Forget it in yours. It's a new day with new dreams. You have been given a whole new life. Start living it!

Satisfaction

"I will refresh the weary
and satisfy the faint."

JEREMIAH 31:25

Satisfaction is the result of a job well done.
Sometimes your expectation for the blessings of God requires you to press a little
harder and stretch your faith a little farther
to see the results you've asked God for. You
can be sure all your effort will be rewarded.
God promises to satisfy your soul—a deep
satisfaction only He can provide. He's given
you the power to reach your destiny. He will
not let you fail. Press on! Press on!

> [The Lord] satisfies me with good
> things and makes me young again,
> like the eagle.
>
> PSALM 103:5 NCV

The enormous wealth of love God has for you compels Him to shower you with His presence and draw you close to Him. The fresh scent that remains after a spring rain shower is an open invitation to rest in His mercy and grace. The flutter of a hummingbird's wings or the gentle sigh from a toddler's crib sends a special message that expresses His gentle desire to satisfy your heart with everything good.

Security

The righteous will never be moved. . . .
Their hearts are firm,
secure in the Lord.

PSALM 112:6–7 NRSV

God is your safe haven from all of life's difficulty. When the pressures of life seem more than you can take—grab hold of the stability found only in Him. You're His for safekeeping. He stands ready to receive you with open arms. The blanket of His love and compassion are there to surround you and bring warmth to your heart during life's coldest hours. Stand under His umbrella of protection throughout the storms. Take refuge in Him—He's your sanctuary!

> Trust in the Lord, and do good;
> so you will live in the land,
> and enjoy security.

PSALM 37:3 NRSV

Throughout history the church building served as a place of sanctuary for criminals and debtors to escape the wrath of those who wanted to pay them back for wrongs done. They could not be touched until they had received due process and were found guilty for their crimes. Jesus offers you asylum in much the same way. He has even paid the penalty for your crimes. His righteousness given to you is your safe place.

Self-Control

Prepare your minds for action;
be self-controlled; set your hope fully
on the grace to be given you when
Jesus Christ is revealed.

1 Peter 1:13

There are moments in every woman's life when her emotions take on a life of their own. When those times come to your life, God wants you to walk by faith and not by sight—being led by confidence in Him rather than your feelings. The gift of self-control will put you in His best light and keep you from responding foolishly. He stands ready to help you choose self-control. Believe in Him because He believes in you.

> Let us be self-controlled,
> putting on faith and love
> as a breastplate, and the
> hope of salvation as a helmet.
>
> 1 THESSALONIANS 5:8

Self-control is the ability to control your own behavior, especially your reactions and impulses. You alone are responsible for your choices, decisions, and actions. God has given you the Holy Spirit to help you live as you were designed to live—a productive, fulfilled life. No matter what others do or say, you have the power to do what is right. God has given you all the tools you need to come out on top.

Serving God

Acknowledge the God of your father,
and serve him with wholehearted
devotion and with a willing mind, for the
LORD searches every heart and understands every motive behind the thoughts.

1 CHRONICLES 28:9

Perhaps God didn't call you to be a mis-
sionary or preach the gospel, yet you are still
called to serve God and it's much easier than
you think. It's simply allowing God in you to
do what He's equipped you to do. If you like to
talk, you may be an encourager. If you like to
bake, perhaps you have the gift of hospitality. Inside you there are blessings
for others waiting to be handed
out. You're serving God day after
day—exactly the way He intended.

Jesus said, "Whoever serves me must follow me; and where I am, my servant also will be. My Father will honor the one who serves me."

JOHN 12:26

Serving God has no limits. Today women can serve God in any way they desire. No calling is too big or too small. Perhaps you're raising the next generation—your own children—to serve God. Maybe you speak to hundreds of thousands through books or on public platforms. Let your faith soar and remove anything that limits you. As you follow God, He will make the impossible, possible. When you think you can, you can.

Singleness

When you're unmarried,
you're free to concentrate
on simply pleasing the Master.

1 CORINTHIANS 7:32 MSG

There is a season for everything on earth—
that includes your singleness. Whether you
remain single throughout your life or choose
one day to marry, this is a special time, a
time when you are free to grow and learn
and draw closer to God. Singleness is full of
treasures. Many singles miss these because
they are focused on the future. Rejoice in
the now. See what God has in store for you
today.

God gives the gift of
the single life to some,
the gift of the married life to others.

1 CORINTHIANS 7:7 MSG

Society can add great pressure to conform to the norm of married life. Take courage in who you are today. God has great plans for you now—not just in the future! He's not waiting on you to get married to fulfill your destiny. Your plan and purpose in life is about YOU! You can boldly live for Him today and trust Him to take care of tomorrow. He's given you everything you need to live a great life. What are you waiting for?

Sleep

I will lie down and sleep in peace,
for you alone,
O LORD, make me dwell in safety.

PSALM 4:8

Strangely, your body was designed like
a battery. It runs down and has to be re-
charged. That's why sleep is so important.
Your body powers down and reaches a point
in which you are fully relaxed. Then you
begin to refuel and rebuild. It's a time of
restoration for your body and your mind.

The Lord has promised you the blessing
of peaceful sleep. You can relax and
take comfort knowing He never
sleeps but watches over you at
all times.

I lie down and sleep; I wake again,
for the Lord sustains me.

PSALM 3:5 NRSV

Fear is the opposite of faith. Sometimes
it comes disguised as worry or despair and
very often it tries to rob you of precious
sleep. The Bible says love casts out all fear
and faith works by love. As you fall
asleep, think of just how much God
loves you. Build your faith by recall-
ing all He has done for you. Count your
blessings instead of sheep; then sleep
peacefully in your heavenly Father's
protective arms.

Speech

A [woman] finds joy in giving an apt
reply—and how good is a timely word!

PROVERBS 15:23

Your life experiences speak of God's
faithfulness and love, and He wants you to
share what He's done for you with others.
Someone out there may be struggling to take
the next step toward God's love and plan for
her life, and you can bring encouragement
by sharing how God helped you through the
tough times. In the process, your own faith
will be strengthened. You have answers. Be
bold and courageous. Speak up!

> Gracious speech is like clover honey—good taste to the soul, quick energy for the body.
>
> PROVERBS 16:24 MSG

Women are quoted throughout the history books for their inspirational speeches and clever wisdom that helped a community, a city, or a nation overcome crisis. At the time they were just sharing a word of encouragement. That same God who inspired them lives inside of you. You can be inspiration to your family, friends, and coworkers. You can provide substance for the souls of those around you. Your words have power.

Spiritual Growth

We, who with unveiled faces all reflect
the Lord's glory, are being transformed
into his likeness with ever-increasing
glory, which comes from the Lord,
who is the Spirit.

2 CORINTHIANS 3:18

Each day, whether you know it or not, you are growing in the Lord, becoming more and more like Him. Simply because His Spirit dwells within you, you are being transformed from the inside out, reflecting the glory of God that burns from within. That's why you will often feel a nudge from deep down inside to deal with a certain issue or let go of a negative thought or behavior. You are literally growing up in God. How wonderful is that!

This is my prayer: that your love
may abound more and more in
knowledge and depth of insight.

PHILIPPIANS 1:9

The Spirit of God works within you to transform you to His image, but you must do your part, as well. Your job is to respond to the work being done inside. You must relinquish sin, build up your spirit by reading God's Word, open your heart to wisdom and counsel, and surrender your old nature to be replaced by your new one. Your spiritual growth is intended to be a collaboration between you and God. The work is often difficult, but it brings great rewards.

Strength

The Lord is my strength, my song,
and my salvation. He is my God,
and I will praise him.

EXODUS 15:2 TLB

In the universe, there is really just one
source of strength—that is God. Others may
be strong for you, on your behalf, but they
cannot impart that strength to you. When
you invite God to fill your heart and life, you
are strengthened from within. His strength
literally becomes your strength. You are em-
powered to do, to stand, to fight, to conquer.
If Christ is there, you don't need to reach
outside yourself for strength. Reach inside
and find all you need.

I can do everything through him
who gives me strength.

PHILIPPIANS 4:13

You're probably busier than you've ever
been—doing more than you've ever done.
Maybe you feel exhausted—physically,
mentally, and emotionally. God has given
you strength for your days—even the tough-
est ones. He is the source you can draw on
when you feel your supply is running low.
You don't have to go at life alone. When you
reach for Him, He's always there, ready to
refresh you. Find quiet moments to dip
your soul into His supply. You'll come away
strengthened and renewed.

Success

Wisdom brings success.
ECCLESIASTES 10:10 NKJV

God has great plans for you. Sometimes your own plans may sound more adventurous or even more profitable than what God has for you. But remember, He sees and knows all—the beginning from the end. He knows the best road to take to get you to your destiny. He sees the obstacles along the way. He sees the eternal as well as the physical. Embrace the future He has for you, and you'll be a true success story.

> [It is not that] we think we can do
> anything of lasting value by ourselves.
> Our only power and success
> come from God.

2 CORINTHIANS 3:5 TLB

God created you for success, but He never planned for you to acquire it alone. You may experience a small measure of success here and there by your own wit, but imagine where you can go in God. True success comes when you're willing to say, "It's not about me and all about You, Lord." Then He is free to take you to a level that you can only achieve with His strength and power propelling you. Then you'll discover lasting success in Him.

Thankfulness

Give thanks to the LORD, for he is good;
his love endures forever.

1 CHRONICLES 16:34

Each of the four seasons—fall, winter, spring, and summer—demonstrate creation's thankfulness to God for a job well done. The trees bow before heaven as their leaves fall gracefully to the ground. The glistening snowfall speaks of God's majesty. Flowers of every kind bow low to the glory God in spring, and summer warms to the glow of all the blessings God has to offer. What has God done for you? Take a moment and express your gratefulness to Him in your own way.

> Thanks be to God,
> which giveth us the victory
> through our Lord Jesus Christ.
>
> 1 CORINTHIANS 15:57 KJV

What a wonderful, giving God we serve. He stands with an extended hand, ready to give you the desires of your heart. Take a moment to offer thanks to Him for the greatest gifts, the awesome joys you've experienced, and even the small things that you realize He engineered to bless you in an unexpected way. Share with Him just how much He means to you. Express to Him your thankfulness. He is worthy of your thanks.

Thoughts

When my anxious thoughts
multiply within me,
Your consolations delight my soul.

PSALM 94:19 NASB

Your thoughts produce your attitudes and
behaviors—your actions. They are, of all your
physical assets, the most powerful. Your
heavenly Father wants you to direct your
thoughts toward life and blessing. The Bible
says to think about those things that are pure,
honest, true, virtuous, lovely, and of a good
report. When you control your thoughts,
they cannot be used by the enemy
of your soul to harass you. Your
thoughts will help you become
free in every aspect of your life.

> We take captive every thought
> to make it obedient to Christ.
>
> 2 CORINTHIANS 10:5

God gave you a creative mind filled with
an amazing ability to think and reason.
Your thoughts are the starting point of every
decision you make and action you take.
Your loving heavenly Father gave you
guidelines in His Word to help you
determine the direction your thoughts
should take. He created you to fulfill
every dream He placed inside you. Think
higher—His way of thinking produces
peace, health, prosperity, wisdom, and
so many blessings.

Trust

Trust the Lord with all your heart,
and don't depend on your
own understanding.

PROVERBS 3:5 NCV

Teammates have to rely on one another to succeed in any endeavor. They have to have a certain level of confidence in one another and their abilities to help them succeed. God trusts you enough to put you on His eternal team. He has confidence in you because He knows you can do all things through Christ, who gives you strength. He chose you to stand alongside your team captain, Jesus, and go to the board for a win!

> "Anyone who trusts in [God]
> will never be put to shame."
>
> ROMANS 10:11

As you look back on the journey you've traveled—recall the times you placed hope and confidence in God. The outcome might not have been exactly as you imagined, but God is always faithful to bring you through. Count each blessing He's given you along the way and consider them stepping-stones to a higher level of trust. Whatever you're facing today, you can rest assured that His blessings will never stop. He will walk it out with you—every step of the way.

Truth

Speaking the truth in love. . .
grow up into him in all things,
which is the head, even Christ.

EPHESIANS 4:15 KJV

Heated words really stress relationships. A white lie may seem more easily swallowed than the blunt truth of a situation, but God has blessed you with the help of His Holy Spirit to bring truth into the lives of others. He knows their hearts and the words that should be spoken to bring them closer to God and to you. Truth mixed with love is a rich treasure, and when it overflows out of your heart, it becomes a beautiful gift to those around you.

Jesus said, "You shall know the truth,
and the truth shall make you free."

JOHN 8:32 NKJV

Jesus is Truth. Like 24-karat gold is pure
gold—without impurities—Jesus is pure
truth. The light and life of God lives in you,
therefore the blessing of truth is always
available to you, helping you know and
discern what is good and right for your
life. Jesus never promised your pathway
would be easy, but He has promised to
never leave you. Truth is always with you.
And you can call upon Him in every
circumstance to light your way.

Waiting

Be strong, and let your heart take
courage, all you who wait for the Lord.

PSALM 31:24 NRSV

God waits for you. You are the precious
fruit of the earth, and like a farmer waits
for harvest, God is waiting for you. Imagine
what it must be like for Him to wait for you
to grow, building trust and confidence in
Him. He offers you spiritual food and
water, believing you will take root and
become strong and confident in His Word
and in your relationship with Him. And to
Him, you're well worth the wait.

If we hope for what we do not see,
we wait for it with patience.

ROMANS 8:25 NRSV

Waiting eventually produces blessing after a time of transition. Consider a woman in labor awaiting the birth of her baby. She's not sitting still—she's experiencing active labor. She's working hard through transition. How exciting to know that what you've asked God for is on its way. As God works behind the scenes to bring about everything you're waiting for, your faith is at work preparing for the arrival of His blessing.

Wholeness

The very God of peace sanctify you
wholly; and I pray God your whole
spirit and soul and body be
preserved blameless unto the
coming of our Lord Jesus Christ.

I THESSALONIANS 5:23 KJV

Human beings—and especially women—are
uniquely complex. Emotions of the soul play on
attitudes of the mind and together impact the
body, which responds with intensity enough to
affect emotions and establish attitudes. That's
why it's important to be wholly surrendered
to God. You must nurture and nourish every
aspect of who you are. Ask God to establish harmony in your life, mind, and
soul conformed to God's ways and a
body that reflects inner peace.

> [Jesus] said unto him, Arise, go thy way:
> thy faith hath made thee whole.
>
> LUKE 17:19 KJV

Wholeness is a faith matter—not necessarily faith that God is going to touch you right here right now, but faith that wholeness of spirit, mind, and body will come as you surrender all aspects of yourself to Him and begin to serve Him. God rarely removes our limitations before we start down the path. Instead, they fall into the background as we get on our way. Ask God to make you whole—completely whole—and then begin living your life to the full.

Wisdom

The Lord gives wisdom;
from his mouth come knowledge
and understanding.

PROVERBS 2:6 NRSV

Have you ever had that feeling deep in your gut that you should—or shouldn't—do something? The Holy Spirit dwells within you, ready to give you the wisdom you need to make good choices for your life. If you're listening, you will hear Him, but He is a gentleman. He won't shout or force you to hear what He has to say. The more you trust His lead, the more you will grow in wisdom.

The fear of the LORD
is the beginning of wisdom;
all who follow his precepts
have good understanding.
To him belongs eternal praise.

PSALM 111:10

When you find yourself in a jam, you don't have to figure it out on your own. God has answers to the questions you ask. You may find wisdom in a scripture that He prompts you to read, an insight in conversation with a friend. You need His wisdom every single day. God stands ready to assist. All you have to do is ask Him for help and then listen for the answer. Be encouraged—God has all the answers you need.

Work

The desires of the diligent
are fully satisfied.

PROVERBS 13:4

Regardless of whether your work is in
an office or in your home or in your home
office, each morning when you open your
eyes, you've got a job to do. God is pleased
when you apply yourself diligently to the
task He's given you. It may be pleasant
work—it may not. Whatever it is, see it as
your gift to your heavenly Father for the day.

Do it as if He were watching your every
step—because He is.

The sleep of a laborer is sweet.

ECCLESIASTES 5:12

It could be that God has asked you to
work in relative obscurity, where no one
sees and no one knows how diligently
you labor. Sometimes you wonder if
what you do really matters—it does.
God will not forget you. He will be
your companion day after day. And
He will reward you one day in front
of everyone. Labor on, child of God.
Sleep well at night knowing that God is
pleased with you.

Scripture Index

Old Testament

Proverbs

Notes

Notes

Notes

Notes

Notes

Notes

Notes

Notes